Contents

A **Listen and repeat.** **B** **Read, trace, and write.**

1.  one
_____

2. two
_____

3. three
_____

4. four
_____

5. five
_____

6.  six
_____

7.  seven
_____

8. eight
_____

9.  ten
_____

10. first first
_____

11.  game
_____

12. what what
_____

C Read and count.

eight first what **first**

eight **what** what

first eight what

first	☐
what	☐
eight	☐

D Listen and number. E Listen, point, and read.

☐ ☐

It is her first TV show.

☐ ☐

There are five teams on the show.

☐

Chickens have two legs.

☐

The winners will get three prizes.

Anna hosts a TV show.

It is a game show.

Anna is happy to be on TV.

It is her first TV show.

There are five teams on the show.

There is one captain for each team.

The first team has two legs.

What has two legs?

Chickens have two legs.

The second team has four legs.
What has four legs?

Bears have four legs.

The third team has six legs.
What has six legs?

Bees have six legs.

The fourth team has eight legs.
What has eight legs?

Spiders have eight legs.

Crabs have ten legs.

What will the winners get?

The winners will get three prizes.

They need to finish a seven-piece puzzle.

Ready set go!

Activities

A **Match, write, and read.**

1.
2.
3.
4.

s◯ven   t◯o   thre◯   te◯

B **Choose and write.**

1.

eight   seven

_____

2.

two   six

_____

3.

game   what

_____

4.

one   four

_____

C Read, circle, and write.

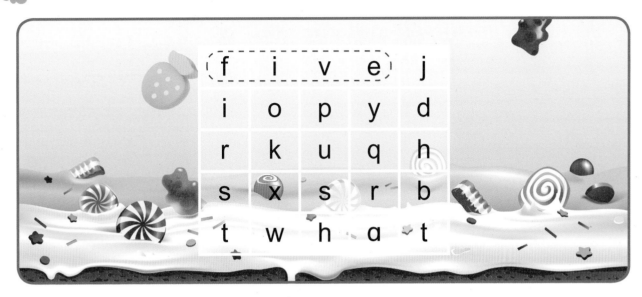

1. five _____
2. four _____
3. what _____
4. first _____

D Place the stickers and write.

1. _____

2. _____

3. _____

4. _____

E Listen, repeat and check three times.

F Read on your own and check 😊 or ☹ .

Can you read?

1. show ⬜⬜⬜   Anna hosts a TV show.   😊 ☹

2. first ⬜⬜⬜   It is her first TV show.   😊 ☹

3. five ⬜⬜⬜   There are five teams on the show.   😊 ☹

4. two ⬜⬜⬜   Chickens have two legs.   😊 ☹

5. four ⬜⬜⬜   Bears have four legs.   😊 ☹

6. six ⬜⬜⬜   Bees have six legs.   😊 ☹

7. eight ⬜⬜⬜   Spiders have eight legs.   😊 ☹

8. ten ⬜⬜⬜   Crabs have ten legs.   😊 ☹

9. three ⬜⬜⬜   The winners will get three prizes.   😊 ☹

10. seven ⬜⬜⬜   They need to finish a seven-piece puzzle.   😊 ☹

G Look, read, and stick. ②

1.

It is her _____ TV show.

2.

Chickens have _____ legs.

3.

Bears have _____ legs.

4.

Bees have _____ legs.

5.

Spiders have _____ legs.

6.

Crabs have _____ legs.

apple best box bread cake corn
day does make take think today

A Listen and repeat. **B** Read, trace, and write. T5

1.  apple _____

2.  best _____

3.  box _____

4.  bread _____

5.  cake _____

6.  corn _____

7. day day _____

8. does does _____

9. make make _____

10. take take _____

11. think think _____

12. today today _____

C Look and draw.

today take does

take today take

take does does does

does = ○

today = △

take = □

D Listen and number. E Listen, point, and read.

☐

She makes vanilla cupcakes.

☐

She makes corn bread.

☐

She makes apple pies.

☐

She makes chocolate cake.

Polly's Bakery

T6

Polly's Bakery

Polly is a baker.

Everyone in town loves Polly's bread.

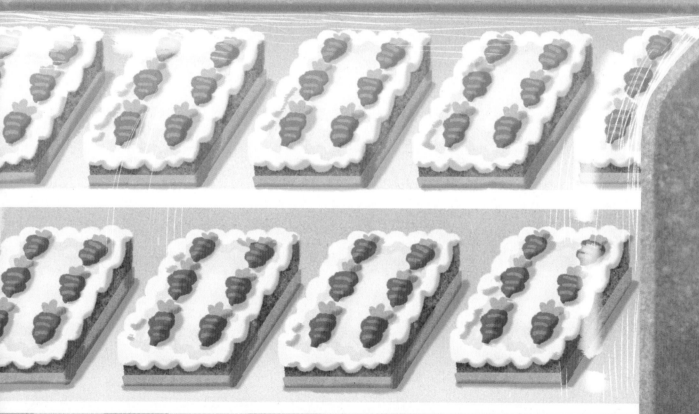

Polly sells one type of bread each day.
Everyone in town thinks Polly is the best.

What does Polly make today?
She makes vanilla cupcakes. They look delicious.

Today's Bread

APPLE PIE! ♡

What does Polly make today?

She makes apple pies. They smell yummy.

What does Polly make today?
She makes corn bread. It smells good.

What does Polly make today?
She makes raisin bread. It looks cute.

What does Polly make today?

She makes strawberry cake. It looks beautiful.

What does Polly make today?
She makes chocolate cake. It smells really good.

Polly's Bakery

Molly's favorite is Polly's chocolate cake.

Molly takes a bus to go to Polly's Bakery.

Polly gives Molly a cake box.
Molly cannot wait to have Polly's yummy cake.

Activities

A Match, trace, and read.

1.

• box •

• cake •

• corn •

• bread •

2.

3.

4.

B Choose and write.

1.

best

make

_____

2.

think

corn

_____

3.

bread

does

_____

4.

make

cake

_____

C. Listen, circle, and write.

best	apple	bread
corn	take	box
make	cake	think
day	today	does

1. She makes raisin _____ .

2. She makes strawberry _____ .

3. Molly _____ s a bus to go to Polly's Bakery.

D. Read and place the stickers. 1

1. Everyone in town loves Polly's _____ .

2. Polly sells one type of bread each _____ .

3. She makes chocolate _____ .

E Listen, repeat and check three times.

F Read on your own and check 😊 or ☹ .

Can you read?

1. bread | Everyone in town loves Polly's bread.

2. day | Polly sells one type of bread each day.

3. does | What does Polly make today?

4. apple | She makes apple pies.

5. corn | She makes corn bread.

6. she | She makes raisin bread.

7. make | She makes strawberry cake.

8. cake | She makes chocolate cake.

9. take | Molly takes a bus to go to Polly's Bakery.

10. box | Polly gives Molly a cake box.

G Find and write the words three times.

1.
2.
3.
4.
5.

light night party robin window sing
good-bye start little off on them

A Listen and repeat.   **B** Read, trace, and write.   T9

1.    light
_____
_ _ _ _ _ _ _
_____

2.   night
_____
_ _ _ _ _ _ _
_____

3.   party
_____
_ _ _ _ _ _ _
_____

4.    robin
_____
_ _ _ _ _ _ _
_____

5.    window
_____
_ _ _ _ _ _ _
_____

6.    sing
_____
_ _ _ _ _ _ _
_____

7.   good-bye   good-bye
_____
_ _ _ _ _ _ _
_____

8.   start   start
_____
_ _ _ _ _ _ _
_____

9.   little   little
_____
_ _ _ _ _ _ _
_____

10.   off   off
_____
_ _ _ _ _ _ _
_____

11.   on   on
_____
_ _ _ _ _ _ _
_____

12.   them   them
_____
_ _ _ _ _ _ _
_____

C Find, match the color, and write.

little   on   little them   on   them   little
on   them   little   little   on

little	them	on
little		

D Listen and number.

Mom turns off the light.

Tyler can see stars through his window.

Ryan, the singing robin, joins the party.

It is time to say good-bye to his friends.

E Listen, point, and read.

☐ ☐

☐

☐ ☐

☐

Tyler's Window

Tyler's mom tells Tyler a bedtime story.
"Good night, Tyler!" Mom turns off the light.

Tyler cannot sleep.

Tyler can see stars through his window.

Tyler's friends come one by one.
Denny, the little dragon, knocks on the window.

Tyler opens the window and welcomes Denny.
Fay, the flying fish, comes through the window.

They start a night party.
Ryan, the singing robin, joins the party.

They turn on music.
Mike, the dancing monkey, cannot miss the party.

They sing together.
Cathy, the talking cat, loves to play with them.

They have so much fun together.
Tyler is happy to have cool friends.

"Tyler, go to sleep!" Mom says.
It is time to say good-bye to his friends.

They do not want to go, but they have to.
Good night and see you tomorrow!

Activities

A **Look and circle two correct words.**

1.

| light | night | light | night |

2.

| them | robin | robin | them |

3.

| party | window | window | party |

4.

| start | sing | sing | start |

B **Choose and write.**

1.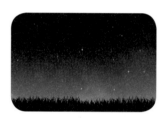

night   light

_____

2.

them   sing

_____

3.

robin   little

_____

4.

window   start

_____

C Look and write.

```
        1
     2
  3    i    g
        
        t
4
```

Down				Across			
1		2		3		4	

D Place the stickers and circle. ①

1.

		t	l	e

little
good-bye

2.

t	h	

off
them

3.

		r	t

start
sing

4.

n	i		t

light
night

F Read on your own and check 😊 or 🙁 .

Can you read?

1. light [ ][ ][ ] Mom turns off the light. 😊 🙁

2. window [ ][ ] Tyler can see stars through his window. 😊 🙁

3. little [ ][ ][ ] Denny, the little dragon, knocks on the window. 😊 🙁

4. come [ ][ ][ ] Fay, the flying fish, comes through the window. 😊 🙁

5. sing [ ][ ] Ryan, the singing robin, joins the party. 😊 🙁

6. party [ ][ ][ ] Mike, the dancing monkey, cannot miss the party. 😊 🙁

7. them [ ][ ][ ] Cathy, the talking cat, loves to play with them. 😊 🙁

8. fun [ ][ ][ ] They have so much fun together. 😊 🙁

9. good-bye [ ][ ][ ] It is time to say good-bye to his friends. 😊 🙁

10. night [ ][ ][ ] Good night and see you tomorrow! 😊 🙁

G Look, follow, and write.

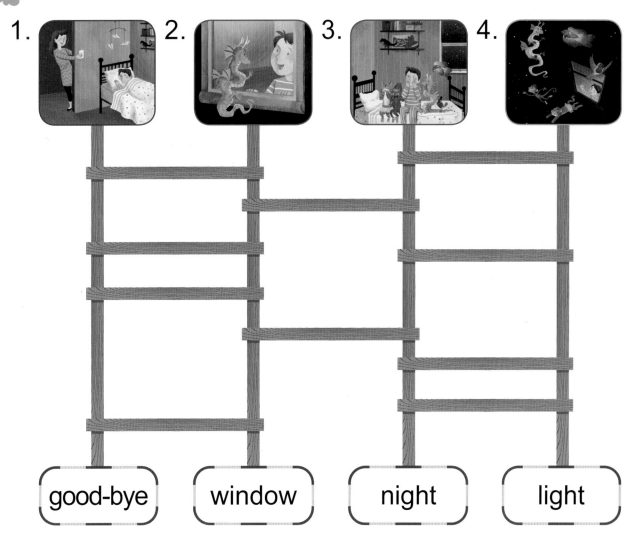

1. good-bye
2. window
3. night
4. light

1. Mom turns off the _____.

2. Denny, the little dragon, knocks on the _____.

3. It is time to say _____ to his friends.

4. Good _____ and see you tomorrow!

Unit 4 Words

A Listen and repeat.

 B Read, trace, and write.   T13

1.  cold
_____

2.  hot
_____

3.  warm
_____

4.  rain
_____

5.  wind
_____

6. been been
_____

7. had had
_____

8. hold hold
_____

9. saw saw
_____

10. around around
_____

11. at at
_____

12. where where
_____

C Find, circle, and count.

1. had
ukhadpqjhadmhadrwedlhad ☐

2. saw
sawrlbsawtkfdgkksawpoivnc ☐

3. been
eudbeengkbeenzdljebeenok ☐

4. hold
mholdsdkjskfjkslholdqchdkk ☐

D Listen and number.   E Listen, point, and read.

☐

It was very hot. We swam at the beach.

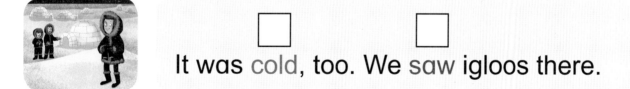

☐   ☐

It was cold, too. We saw igloos there.

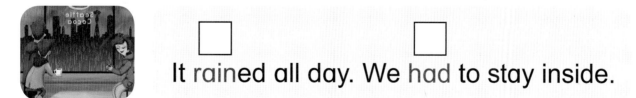

☐   ☐

It rained all day. We had to stay inside.

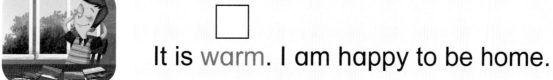

☐

It is warm. I am happy to be home.

Where did you go?

I have been all around the world.

Tell me where you have been.
What was the weather like?

We went to Mexico.

It was very hot. We swam at the beach.

We went to Kenya.

It was hot, too. We had fun on a wildlife safari.

We went to Switzerland.

It was very cold. We skied down a mountain.

We went to Alaska, U.S.A.

It was cold, too. We saw igloos there.

We went to Seattle, U.S.A.

It rained all day. We had to stay inside.

We went to Wellington, New Zealand.

It was very windy. We had to hold our jackets.

I am happy to come back home.
It is not too cold. It is not too hot.

It does not rain a lot. It is not too windy.
It is warm. I am happy to be home.

Activities

A Look and write.

1. where   w h ere   w ere   w e re

2. around   a ound   ar und   arou d

3. hold   h ld   ho d   hol

4. warm   w rm   wa m   war

B Choose and write.

1.

   wind

   where

2.

   saw

   rain

3.

   hold

   hot

4.

   cold

   at

C Read and draw.

been = △	hold = ○	around = □	saw = ☆

saw	around	hold	saw
around	been	saw	hold
hold	saw	hold	been
around	been	saw	around

D Listen, circle, and place the stickers. ❶

1.

hot	had

h	

2.

rain	around

aro	

3.

at	been

be	

4.

warm	where

	ere

F **Read on your own and check 😊 or 🙁.**

Can you read?

1. been — I have been all around the world. 😊 🙁

2. what — What was the weather like? 😊 🙁

3. at — It was very hot. We swam at the beach. 😊 🙁

4. had — It was hot, too. We had fun on a wildlife safari. 😊 🙁

5. cold — It was very cold. We skied down a mountain. 😊 🙁

6. saw — It was cold, too. We saw igloos there. 😊 🙁

7. rain — It rained all day. We had to stay inside. 😊 🙁

8. wind — It was very windy. We had to hold our jackets. 😊 🙁

9. hot — It is not too cold. It is not too hot. 😊 🙁

10. warm — It is warm. I am happy to be home. 😊 🙁

G Look, number, and stick. ②

It was hot, too. We _____ fun on a wildlife safari.

It is not too cold. It is not too _____ .

It was very _____ . We skied down a mountain.

I have been all _____ the world.

What _____ the weather like?

It was very windy. We had to _____ our jackets.

Review

 Check the words you can read.

☐ apple ☐ eight ☐ night ☐ take

☐ around ☐ first ☐ off ☐ ten

☐ at ☐ five ☐ on ☐ them

☐ been ☐ four ☐ one ☐ think

☐ best ☐ game ☐ party ☐ three

☐ box ☐ good-bye ☐ rain ☐ today

☐ bread ☐ had ☐ robin ☐ two

☐ cake ☐ hold ☐ saw ☐ warm

☐ cold ☐ hot ☐ seven ☐ what

☐ corn ☐ light ☐ sing ☐ where

☐ day ☐ little ☐ six ☐ wind

☐ does ☐ make ☐ start ☐ window

Play the board game. Read the words.

FINISH ★	25 **7**	24 night	23 Go Back 2 Spaces → eight	
18 been →	19 [window]	20 make	21 take	22 [birthday party]
17 go	16 had	Go Back 2 Spaces	15 where ←	14 does
9 first →	10 little	11 **6**	12 wind	13 day
8 one	Go Back 2 Spaces	7 hot	6 **10** ←	5 did
START →	1 what	2 come	3 off	4 [box]

Answer Key

Unit 1

p. 3

C first - 3, what - 4, eight - 3

D

⑤ ③ It is her first TV show.

④ ⑥ There are five teams on the show.

① Chickens have two legs.

② The winners will get three prizes.

p. 14

A

1. 10 2. (puzzle) 3. 7 4. 3

seven · two · three · ten

B 1. eight 2. six 3. game 4. one

p. 15

C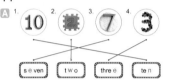

f i v e j
i o p y d
r k u q h
s x s r b
t w h a t

1. five — five   2. four — four
3. what — what   4. first — first

D 1. game   2. five   3. eight   4. seven

p. 17

G 1. It is her first TV show.
2. Chickens have two legs.
3. Bears have four legs.
4. Bees have six legs.
5. Spiders have eight legs.
6. Crabs have ten legs.

Unit 2

p. 19

C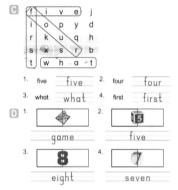

does = ○
today = △
take = □

D ③ She makes vanilla cupcakes.

① She makes corn bread.

② She makes apple pies.

④ She makes chocolate cake.

p. 30

A 1. corn → bread   2. (hand/bread)
3. (berries) → cake / corn   4. box

B 1. best   2. corn
3. bread   4. cake

p. 31

C

best   apple   (bread)
corn   (take)   box
make   (cake)   think
day   today   does

1. She makes raisin bread.
2. She makes strawberry cake.
3. Molly take s a bus to go to Polly's Bakery.

D 1. Everyone in town loves Polly's bread.
2. Polly sells one type of bread each day.
3. She makes chocolate cake.

p. 33

G 1. apple   2. best   3. does
4. bread   5. cake   * 번호순서무관

Unit 3

p. 35

C

little   them   on
little   on
little   them   on
little   on
little   them
little   them   on

D ③ ⑥ Mom turns off the light.

① Tyler can see stars through his window.

② ④ Ryan, the singing robin, joins the party.

⑤ It is time to say good-bye to his friends.

p. 46

A 1. light   2. robin
3. party   4. sing   *각 번호당 2개씩

B 1. night   2. sing
3. robin   4. window

p. 47

C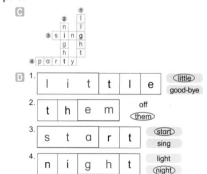

1. little
2. them
3. sing
4. party

D 1. l i t t l e   (little / good-bye)
2. t h e m   (off / them)
3. s t a r t   (start / sing)
4. n i g h t   (light / night)

p. 49

G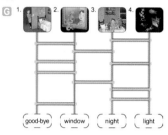

1. 2. 3. 4.

good-bye   window   night   light

1. Mom turns off the light.
2. Denny, the little dragon, knocks on the window.
3. It is time to say good-bye to his friends.
4. Good night and see you tomorrow!

Unit 4

p. 51

C 1. had   ukhadpqhadmhadrwedhad   ④
2. saw   sawlbsawtkfdgklsawpoivnc   ③
3. been   eudbeenglheenzdljpbeenok   ①
4. hold   mholdsdkjskfjkqholdnchdkk   ②

D ④ It was very hot. We swam at the beach.

① ⑥ It was cold, too. We saw igloos there.

③ ② It rained all day. We had to stay inside.

⑤ It is warm. I am happy to be home.

p. 62

B 1. wind   2. rain   3. hot   4. cold

p. 63

C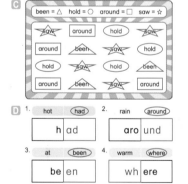

been = △   hold = ○   around = □   saw = ☆

saw   around   hold   saw
around   been   saw   hold
hold   saw   hold   been
around   been   saw   around

D 1. hot (had)   h ad
2. rain (around)   aro und
3. at (been)   be en
4. warm (where)   wh ere

p. 65

G 3 – It was hot, too. We had fun on a wildlife safari.

6 – It is not too cold. It is not too hot.

4 – It was very cold. We skied down a mountain.

1 - I have been all around the world.

2 – What was the weather like?

5 – It was very windy. We had to hold our jackets.

68 Answer Key

1

| 5 | 7 | 18 | 8 |

2   six   two   four   eight   first   ten

1   cake   day   bread

1

| l | i | t | | e | m |

| s | t | a | | g | h |

1

| wh | ad |

| en | und |

2   was   cold

had   around

hot   hold